Easy Spring Roll Cookbook

50 Delicious Spring Roll and Egg Roll Recipes

By
Chef Maggie Chow
Copyright © by Saxonberg Associates
All rights reserved

Published by
BookSumo, a division of Saxonberg Associates
http://www.booksumo.com/

INTRODUCTION

Welcome to *The Effortless Chef Series*! Thank you for taking the time to download the *Easy Spring Roll Cookbook*. Come take a journey with me into the delights of easy cooking. The point of this cookbook and all my cookbooks is to exemplify the effortless nature of cooking simply.

In this book we focus on Spring Rolls. You will find that even though the recipes are simple, the taste of the dishes is quite amazing.

So will you join me in an adventure of simple cooking? If the answer is yes (and I hope it is) please consult the table of contents to find the dishes you are most interested in. Once you are ready jump right in and start cooking.

— Chef Maggie Chow

Table of Contents

Introduction 2

Table of Contents 3

Any Issues? Contact Me 7

Legal Notes 8

Common Abbreviations 9

Chapter 1: Easy Spring Roll Recipes 10

    Banana & Brown Sugar Spring Rolls 10

    Chicken & Veggies Spring Rolls 12

    Pork & Veggies Spring Rolls 14

    Shrimp & Veggies Spring Rolls with Dipping Sauce 17

    Chicken, Crab & Veggie Spring Rolls 19

    Chicken & Bell Pepper Spring Rolls with Caesar Dressing ... 22

    Shrimp & Vermicelli Spring Rolls with Sauces 24

    Fruit & Sushi Rice Spring Rolls 27

Veggie & Noodles Spring Rolls with Creamy Sauce 30

Creamy Spring Rolls 33

Mixed Meat & Cabbage Spring Rolls....................................... 35

Turkey & Veggie Spring Rolls 38

Radishes, Cucumber & Cabbage Spring Rolls....................... 40

Gingered Shrimp & Veggie Spring Rolls 43

Wine Braised Veggie Spring Rolls.. 46

Sweet Pumpkin Spring Rolls.. 49

Cheesy Beef Spring Rolls with Honey Mustard Sauce 51

Pork & Crab Spring Rolls 54

Chicken, Shrimp & Veggie Spring Rolls 56

Cabbage & Carrot Spring Rolls 59

Chicken & Ham Spring Rolls 61

Herbed Tuna Spring Rolls with Tangy Sauce......................... 64

Veggie & Thread Noodles Spring Rolls with Mustard Sauce. 66

Salmon Spring Rolls with Spicy Mayo 69

Sausage Rolls in Sweet Nutty Glaze 72

Indian Spring Rolls 74

Spicy Beef Spring Rolls 76

Beef & Carrot Spring Rolls 79

Cinnamon Apple Spring Rolls with Coffee Sauce 81

Pumpkin Egg Rolls with Creamy Filling 84

Cheesy Chicken Spring Rolls 87

Mango & Veggie Spring Rolls with Creamy Sauce 90

Spring Roll Noodle Salad with Shrimp 93

Chocolaty Banana Spring Rolls 96

Spicy Beef & Shrimp Spring Rolls 98

Creamy Turkey Lettuce Rolls 101

Tangy Chicken, Apple & Veggie Spring Rolls 103

Braised Eggplant Rolls 106

Cheesy Asparagus Bread Spring Rolls 109

Vegan Spring Rolls with Tangy Sauce 111

Shrimp & Rice Noodles Spring Rolls 114

Steamed Tempeh & Veggie Spring Rolls 117

Soy Sauce Tuna Spring Rolls 119

Chocolaty Peanut Spring Rolls 121

Chicken & Mushroom Spring Rolls 123

Sweetcorn & Crab Spring Rolls with Sweet & Spicy Sauce .. 126

Strawberry & Orange Spring Rolls with Strawberry Sauce . 129

Filipino Style Spring Rolls 132

Veggie Spring Rolls with Spicy Sauce 135

Strawberry & Banana Spring Rolls 137

THANKS FOR READING! NOW LET'S TRY SOME **SUSHI** AND **DUMP DINNERS**.. 139

Come On 141

Let's Be Friends :) 141

Can I Ask A Favour? 142

Interested in Other Easy Cookbooks? 143

ANY ISSUES? CONTACT ME

If you find that something important to you is missing from this book please contact me at maggie@booksumo.com.

I will try my best to re-publish a revised copy taking your feedback into consideration and let you know when the book has been revised with you in mind.

:)

— Chef Maggie Chow

Legal Notes

ALL RIGHTS RESERVED. NO PART OF THIS BOOK MAY BE REPRODUCED OR TRANSMITTED IN ANY FORM OR BY ANY MEANS. PHOTOCOPYING, POSTING ONLINE, AND / OR DIGITAL COPYING IS STRICTLY PROHIBITED UNLESS WRITTEN PERMISSION IS GRANTED BY THE BOOK'S PUBLISHING COMPANY. LIMITED USE OF THE BOOK'S TEXT IS PERMITTED FOR USE IN REVIEWS WRITTEN FOR THE PUBLIC AND/OR PUBLIC DOMAIN.

COMMON ABBREVIATIONS

C.(s)	C.
tbsp	tbsp
tsp	tsp
oz.	oz.
lb	lb

*All units used are standard American measurements

Chapter 1: Easy Spring Roll Recipes

Banana & Brown Sugar Spring Rolls

Ingredients

- 2 large bananas
- 8 (7 inch square) spring roll wrappers
- 1 C. brown sugar, or to taste
- 1 quart oil for deep frying

Directions

- In a large cast-iron skillet or deep fryer, heat the oil to 375 degrees F.
- Slice the bananas in half lengthwise and cut into fourths crosswise.
- Arrange 1 piece of banana over the corner of a spring roll wrapper diagonally and sprinkle with brown sugar.
- Roll the each corner of the wrapper to the center and fold bottom and top corners in and continue rolling.
- With your wet fingers brush the edges of the wrapper to seal the roll.
- Carefully, add the banana rolls in the skillet in batches.
- Fry the rolls till golden brown and transfer onto paper towel lined plates to drain.

Amount per serving (8 total)

Timing Information:

Preparation	10 m
Cooking	10 m
Total Time	20 m

Nutritional Information:

Calories	325 kcal
Fat	11.6 g
Carbohydrates	53.3g
Protein	3.5 g
Cholesterol	3 mg
Sodium	191 mg

* Percent Daily Values are based on a 2,000 calorie diet.

Chicken & Veggies Spring Rolls

Ingredients

- 1 quart oil for deep frying
- 2 (10 oz.) cans chunk chicken, drained and flaked
- 1 small onion, grated
- 1/2 C. finely shredded cabbage
- 1 small carrot, grated
- 1/4 C. barbeque sauce
- 1 dash hot pepper sauce
- 1 dash soy sauce
- 1 dash Worcestershire sauce
- 1 (14 oz.) package spring roll wrappers

Directions

- In a large cast-iron skillet or deep fryer, heat the oil to 375 degrees F.
- In a large bowl, mix together all the ingredients except wrappers.
- Divide chicken mixture in the center of each wrapper.
- Roll the wrapper around the filling and with your wet fingers brush the edges and press to seal completely.
- Carefully, add the rolls in the skillet in batches.
- Fry the rolls for about 5 minutes or till golden brown and transfer onto paper towel lined plates to drain.

Amount per serving (10 total)

Timing Information:

Preparation	30 m
Cooking	15 m
Total Time	45 m

Nutritional Information:

Calories	299 kcal
Fat	13.9 g
Carbohydrates	26.3g
Protein	16.2 g
Cholesterol	38 mg
Sodium	587 mg

* Percent Daily Values are based on a 2,000 calorie diet.

Pork & Veggies Spring Rolls

Ingredients

- 1/2 lb ground pork
- 1 C. finely shredded cabbage
- 1/4 C. finely shredded carrot
- 2 green onions, thinly sliced
- 2 tbsps chopped fresh cilantro
- 1/2 tsp sesame oil
- 1/2 tbsp oyster sauce
- 2 tsps grated fresh ginger root
- 1 1/2 tsps minced garlic
- 1 tsp chile sauce
- 1 tbsp cornstarch
- 1 tbsp water
- 12 (7 inch square) spring roll wrappers
- 4 tsps vegetable oil

Directions

- Set your oven to 425 degrees F before doing anything else.
- Heat a medium pan on medium-high heat and cook the pork till browned and transfer into a large bowl, after draining the fat.
- Add carrot, cabbage, scallion, garlic, ginger, cilantro, sauces and sesame oil and mix till well combined.
- In a small bowl, mix together water and cornstarch and keep aside.
- Divide the chicken mixture in the center of each wrapper.
- Roll the wrappers around the filling and fold the edges inwards to seal.
- Dip your fingers in cornstarch mixture and brush the edges to seal.
- Coat the rolls with oil and place in a baking dish in a single layer.

- Cook everything in the oven for about 20 minutes or till golden brown, flipping once after 10 minutes.

Amount per serving (12 total)

Timing Information:

Preparation	25 m
Cooking	20 m
Total Time	45 m

Nutritional Information:

Calories	154 kcal
Fat	4.9 g
Carbohydrates	20.1g
Protein	6.7 g
Cholesterol	15 mg
Sodium	201 mg

* Percent Daily Values are based on a 2,000 calorie diet.

Shrimp & Veggies Spring Rolls with Dipping Sauce

Ingredients

- 6 spring roll wrappers
- 12 medium shrimp, cooked and shelled
- 1 C. shredded leaf lettuce
- 1/3 C. chopped cilantro
- 1/2 C. peeled, seeded, chopped cucumber
- 1 medium carrot, julienned
- Quick Thai Dipping Sauce:
- 1 tbsp light soy sauce
- 1 tbsp white-wine vinegar or rice vinegar
- 3 tbsps mirin
- 1/4 tsp grated ginger root (optional)

Directions

- Soak the wrappers, one by one in a bowl of chilled water till limp and transfer onto a smooth surface. In the center of each wrapper, place lettuce, followed by shrimp, cucumber, carrot and cilantro evenly. Roll the wrapper around the filling and with your wet fingers brush the edges and press to seal completely.
- Place the wrappers onto a large plate and with plastic wrap, cover the rolls and refrigerate before serving.
- Meanwhile for the dipping sauce in a bowl mix together all the ingredients.
- Serve the rolls with sauce.

Amount per serving (6 total)

Timing Information:

Preparation	20 m
Cooking	30 m
Total Time	50 m

Nutritional Information:

Calories	59 kcal
Fat	0.3 g
Carbohydrates	8.9g
Protein	3.4 g
Cholesterol	20 mg
Sodium	168 mg

* Percent Daily Values are based on a 2,000 calorie diet.

Chicken, Crab & Veggie Spring Rolls

Ingredients

- 1 quart oil for frying
- 2 tbsps vegetable oil
- 1/3 C. shredded cabbage
- 1/4 C. shredded carrots
- 1/4 C. shredded cucumber
- 2 tbsps diced onion
- 1/4 C. diced green onion
- 2 tbsps finely chopped shiitake mushrooms
- 1/3 C. sun-dried tomatoes, chopped
- salt and pepper to taste
- 2 oz. boneless chicken breast halves, cooked and diced
- 1 oz. cooked crabmeat, diced
- 1 tsp Chinese five-spice powder
- 1 avocado - peeled, pitted and diced
- 1 tsp lemon juice
- 8 spring roll wrappers

Directions

- In a large cast-iron skillet or deep fryer, heat the oil on medium-high heat.
- In another skillet, heat vegetable oil on medium heat and cook the vegetables with salt and black pepper for about 10 minutes.
- Add crabmeat, chicken and five-spice powder and stir to combine.
- Drizzle the avocado with lemon juice and mix it with the chicken mixture.
- Divide the chicken mixture in the center of each wrapper evenly.

- Roll the wrapper around the filling and with your wet fingers brush the edges and press to seal completely.
- Carefully, add the rolls in the skillet in batches.
- Fry the rolls for about 3 minutes or till golden brown and transfer onto paper towel lined plates to drain.

Amount per serving (8 total)

Timing Information:

Preparation	20 m
Cooking	25 m
Total Time	45 m

Nutritional Information:

Calories	208 kcal
Fat	18.8 g
Carbohydrates	7.3g
Protein	4 g
Cholesterol	8 mg
Sodium	71 mg

* Percent Daily Values are based on a 2,000 calorie diet.

Chicken & Bell Pepper Spring Rolls with Caesar Dressing

Ingredients

- 12 rice wrappers (8.5 inch diameter)
- 1 (5 oz.) package baby romaine lettuce leaves
- 1 cooked boneless chicken breast half, sliced into thin strips
- 1 red bell pepper, sliced
- 1/2 C. Caesar salad dressing

Directions

- Soak the wrappers, one by one in a bowl of water till soft and transfer onto a smooth surface.
- In the center of each wrapper, place some lettuce, followed by chicken strips and bell pepper evenly.
- Fold the inner sides of the wrappers around the filling and roll tightly.
- Cut each roll in half and serve with Caesar dressing.

Amount per serving (4 total)

Timing Information:

Preparation	25 m
Cooking	25 m
Total Time	25 m

Nutritional Information:

Calories	230 kcal
Fat	13.8 g
Carbohydrates	15.9g
Protein	9.6 g
Cholesterol	28 mg
Sodium	327 mg

* Percent Daily Values are based on a 2,000 calorie diet.

Shrimp & Vermicelli Spring Rolls with Sauces

Ingredients

For Rolls:

- 2-oz. rice vermicelli
- 8 (8 1/2-inch) rice wrappers
- 8 large cooked shrimp, peeled, deveined and halved
- 3 tbsps fresh cilantro, chopped
- 3 tbsps fresh mint leaves
- 1 1/3 tbsps fresh Thai basil leaves, chopped
- 2 lettuce leaves, chopped

For Sauces:

- 1 tsp peanuts, chopped finely
- 3 tbsps hoisin sauce
- 1/4 C. water
- 2 tbsps white sugar
- 1 garlic clove, minced
- 2 tbsps fresh lime juice
- 1/2 tsp garlic chili sauce

Directions

- In a pan of boiling water, add the vermicelli and cook for about 3-5 minutes or till desired doneness. Drain well.
- Soak the wrappers, one by one in a bowl of warm water for 1 second or till soft and transfer onto a smooth surface.

- In the center of each wrapper, place the shrimp, followed by the vermicelli, fresh herbs and lettuce evenly.
- Fold the inner sides of the wrappers around the filling and roll tightly.
- Meanwhile for first sauce in a bowl mix together the peanuts and hoisin sauce.
- In another bowl mix together the remaining ingredients.
- Serve these rolls with both sauces.

Amount per serving (8 total)

Timing Information:

Preparation	45 m
Cooking	5 m
Total Time	50 m

Nutritional Information:

Calories	82 kcal
Fat	0.7 g
Carbohydrates	15.8g
Protein	3.3 g
Cholesterol	11 mg
Sodium	305 mg

* Percent Daily Values are based on a 2,000 calorie diet.

Fruit & Sushi Rice Spring Rolls

Ingredients

- 2 large fresh peaches
- 1 3/4 C. water
- 1 C. short-grain sushi rice
- 3 1/2 tbsps cream of coconut
- 1 pinch salt
- 10 rice paper wrappers
- 1 C. plum preserves
- 2 C. sliced fresh strawberries
- 2 large seedless oranges, peeled and sectioned
- 1 large grapefruit, peeled and sectioned
- 1/4 C. fresh mint leaves, or as desired
- 1 C. vanilla yogurt, or more to taste (optional)

Directions

- In a large pan of boiling water, cook the peaches for about 1 minute and immediately transfer into a bowl of chilled water for several minutes.
- Remove the peaches from the water and, peel, core and cut the peaches into wedges and keep aside.
- In a pan, mix together the rice, water, coconut cream and salt and bring to a boil and reduce the heat to medium-low.
- Simmer, covered for about 20-25 minutes or till the liquid is absorbed
- Remove everything from the heat and keep aside, uncovered to cool completely.

- Soak the wrappers, one by one in a bowl of chilled water till soft and transfer onto a smooth surface.
- In the center of each wrapper, place rice, followed by plum reserves, strawberries, peaches, oranges, grapefruit and mint.
- Roll the wrapper around the filling and with your wet fingers brush the edges and press to seal completely.
- Cut each roll in half and serve with yogurt.

Amount per serving (10 total)

Timing Information:

Preparation	40 m
Cooking	20 m
Total Time	1 h

Nutritional Information:

Calories	267 kcal
Fat	1.7 g
Carbohydrates	60.7g
Protein	3.7 g
Cholesterol	1 mg
Sodium	61 mg

* Percent Daily Values are based on a 2,000 calorie diet.

Veggie & Noodles Spring Rolls with Creamy Sauce

Ingredients

For Rolls:

- 4-oz. dry rice noodles
- 1 C. red cabbage, shredded
- 2 carrots, peeled and julienned
- 1 English cucumber, peeled and julienned
- 1 red bell pepper, seeded and julienned
- 16 fresh mint leaves
- 16 fresh basil leaves
- 2 avocados, peeled, pitted and sliced thinly
- 16 rice paper sheets

For Sauce:

- 1/2 C. unsweetened coconut milk
- 1/2 C. creamy peanut butter
- 2 tbsps fresh lime juice
- 2 tbsps soy sauce
- 2 tsps hot sauce
- 1/2 tsp sesame oil, toasted
- 1 garlic clove, minced

Directions

- In a large pan of boiling water, cook the noodles according to the package's directions.
- In a large bowl, mix together all the vegetables and fresh herbs.

- Soak the rice papers in a bowl of warm water till soft and transfer onto a smooth surface.
- In the center of each rice paper, place the vegetable mixture, followed by the rice noodles and avocado evenly.
- Roll the papers, one by one around the filling and with your wet fingers brush the edges and press to seal completely.
- In a large bowl, add all the sauce ingredients and mix till well combined.
- Cut each roll in half and serve with sauce.

Amount per serving (8 total)

Timing Information:

Preparation	30 m
Cooking	20 m
Total Time	50 m

Nutritional Information:

Calories	292 kcal
Fat	16.4 g
Carbohydrates	32.2g
Protein	7.6 g
Cholesterol	0 mg
Sodium	403 mg

* Percent Daily Values are based on a 2,000 calorie diet.

Creamy Spring Rolls

Ingredients

- 15 (7 inch square) egg roll wrappers
- 5 tbsps mayonnaise
- 2 mangos - peeled, seeded, and cut into thin strips
- 1 egg white, beaten
- 4 C. canola oil for deep frying

Directions

- In a large cast-iron skillet or deep fryer, heat the oil to 375 degrees F.
- Arrange the wrappers onto a smooth surface and place mayonnaise over the center of each wrapper.
- Arrange the mango slices over the mayonnaise evenly.
- Roll the wrapper around the filling and soak your fingers in egg whites and brush the edges and press to seal completely.
- Fry the rolls for about 4 minutes or till golden brown and transfer onto paper towel lined plates to drain.

Amount per serving (15 total)

Timing Information:

Preparation	30 m
Cooking	20 m
Total Time	50 m

Nutritional Information:

Calories	192 kcal
Fat	10.1 g
Carbohydrates	22.1g
Protein	3.5 g
Cholesterol	5 mg
Sodium	213 mg

* Percent Daily Values are based on a 2,000 calorie diet.

Mixed Meat & Cabbage Spring Rolls

Ingredients

Filling:

- 1/4 lb raw pork, shredded
- 1 raw chicken breast half, shredded
- 1/2 lb raw small shrimp or 1/2 lb shrimp, cut into small pieces
- 1/2 head cabbage, shredded
- 8 -10 dried Chinese mushrooms, soak in boiling water, stems removed & shredded
- 3 scallions, shredded

Sauce:

- 1/3 C. chicken stock
- 1/2 tbsp salt (to taste)
- 3 tbsps dry sherry
- 1 tbsp sugar
- vegetable oil, to stir fry and deep fry
- cornstarch, mixed with water to use as binder
- 1 tbsp sesame oil
- beaten egg
- egg roll wraps or egg roll wrap

Directions

- In a skillet, heat 2 tbsps of oil on high heat and cook the pork till browned.
- Stir in the chicken and cook till browned.
- Stir in the shrimp and cook till desired doneness.
- Drain the fat and transfer the meat mixture into a bowl.
- In the same skillet, heat a little oil and sauté scallion for about 1 minute.

- Stir in mushrooms and cabbage and cook for about 2-3 minutes.
- Add broth, sherry, sugar and salt and stir to combine and bring to a boil.
- Add the cornstarch mixture, stirring continuously.
- Stir in the sesame oil and cooked meat and remove from heat.
- Drain the oil and keep aside to cool completely.
- In a large cast-iron skillet or deep fryer, heat the oil to 325 degrees F.
- Divide the meat mixture in the center of each wrapper.
- Roll the wrapper around the filling and soak your fingers in egg whites and brush the edges and press to seal completely.
- Carefully, add the rolls in the skillet in batches.
- Fry the rolls till golden brown and transfer onto paper towel lined plates to drain.

Amount per serving: 1

Timing Information:

Preparation	1 hr
Total Time	1 hr 30 mins

Nutritional Information:

Calories	113.6
Cholesterol	51.5mg
Sodium	454.2mg
Carbohydrates	5.8g
Protein	11.6g

* Percent Daily Values are based on a 2,000 calorie diet.

Turkey & Veggie Spring Rolls

Ingredients

- 20 large spring roll wrappers
- 6 C. finely shredded cabbage
- 2 large carrots, peeled and grated
- 1 lb lean ground turkey or 1 lb ground lean pork
- 2 tbsps peeled minced fresh ginger
- 1 tbsp toasted sesame oil
- 1/2 tsp salt
- vegetable oil, for brushing

Directions

- Set your oven to 350 degrees F before doing anything else and grease a baking pan.
- In a skillet, heat sesame oil and add the turkey, ginger and salt and cook till done completely.
- Transfer the turkey into a bowl, leaving the fat in the skillet.
- Now, in the same skillet, cook till just tender.
- Transfer the mixture into the bowl with the turkey mixture and let it cool.
- Divide the turkey mixture in the center of each wrapper.
- Roll the wrapper around the filling and soak your fingers in water and brush the edges and press to seal completely.
- Arrange the rolls on the prepared baking pan in a single layer.
- Cook everything in the oven for about 30 minutes or till golden brown.

Amount per serving: 1

Timing Information:

| Preparation | 45 mins |
| Total Time | 1 hr 15 mins |

Nutritional Information:

Calories	141.4
Cholesterol	20.8mg
Sodium	271.3mg
Carbohydrates	20.5g
Protein	7.4g

* Percent Daily Values are based on a 2,000 calorie diet.

Radishes, Cucumber & Cabbage Spring Rolls

Ingredients

- 1/2 C. shredded daikon radishes
- 2 green onions, sliced thin
- 2 tbsps rice vinegar
- 1 tsp Splenda sugar substitute
- 1 small fresh jalapenos, chopped
- 1/2 tsp toasted sesame oil
- 1/2 C. shredded carrot
- 1/2 C. short thin strips cucumber
- 2 tbsps snipped fresh cilantro
- 1 tbsp reduced sodium soy sauce
- 6 rice paper sheets
- 1 1/2 C. bean sprouts
- cilantro
- shredded carrot

Directions

- In a large bowl, mix together the green onions, radishes, jalapeno, rice vinegar, sesame oil and Splenda.
- In another bowl, mix together the cucumber, carrot, cilantro and soy sauce.
- Cover both bowls and refrigerate for about 2-24 hours, stirring once and drain them completely.
- Soak the rice papers, one by one in a bowl of warm water till soft and transfer onto paper towels.

- Place the rice papers onto a smooth surface.
- In the center of each rice paper, place the bean sprouts, followed by the radishes mixture and cucumber mixture evenly.
- Fold the inner sides of rice papers around the filling and roll tightly.
- Arrange the rolls onto a baking dish and cover with a damp towel.
- Refrigerate for about 2 hours before serving.
- Cut each roll in half and serve with a garnishing of carrot and cilantro.

Amount per serving: 12

Timing Information:

Preparation	20 m
Total Time	50 m

Nutritional Information:

Calories	9.9
Cholesterol	0.0mg
Sodium	48.9mg
Carbohydrates	1.7g
Protein	0.5g

* Percent Daily Values are based on a 2,000 calorie diet.

Gingered Shrimp & Veggie Spring Rolls

Ingredients

- 2 tsps olive oil
- 1 1/2 C. green onions, chopped
- 1 tsp garlic, minced
- 1 1/2 tsps fresh ginger, minced
- 2 C. bean sprouts
- 2 C. cabbage, shredded
- 3/4 C. carrot, peeled and julienned
- 3 tbsps oyster sauce
- 1/2 tsp soy sauce
- 14 tsp red pepper flakes, crushed
- 1 1/2 C. large shrimp, peeled, deveined and chopped
- 12 egg roll wraps
- Canola oil, as required

Directions

- In a large skillet, heat olive oil and sauté the green onions, garlic, ginger, bean sprouts, cabbage and carrot till just softened.
- Stir in oyster sauce, soy sauce and red pepper flakes and sauté for about 2 minutes.
- Stir in shrimp and immediately, Remove everything from the heat and let it cool.
- Place the wrappers onto a smooth surface.
- Divide the shrimp mixture in the center of each wrapper evenly.
- Roll the wrappers around the filling and with your wet fingers brush the edges and press to seal completely.

- In a large cast-iron skillet or deep fryer, heat the oil to 350 degrees F.
- Carefully, add the rolls in the skillet in batches.
- Fry the rolls till golden brown and transfer onto paper towel lined plates to drain.

Amount per serving: 12

Timing Information:

Preparation	25 mins
Total Time	29 mins

Nutritional Information:

Calories	111.0
Cholesterol	2.8mg
Sodium	329.9mg
Carbohydrates	22.4g
Protein	4.2g

* Percent Daily Values are based on a 2,000 calorie diet.

Wine Braised Veggie Spring Rolls

Ingredients

- 2 tsps vegetable oil
- 2/3 C. bamboo shoots, sliced thinly
- 1 C. bean sprouts
- 2 carrots, peeled and julienned
- 1 1/2 C. mushrooms, chopped
- 1 bunch scallion, sliced thinly
- 1 tbsp rice wine
- 1 tbsp light soy sauce
- 1 tsp light brown sugar
- Salt, to taste
- 20 egg roll wraps
- 1 tbsp cornstarch paste
- Oil, as required

Directions

- In a large skillet, heat vegetable oil and stir fry the veggies for about 1 minute.
- Stir in wine, soy sauce, sugar and salt and stir fry for about 2 minutes.
- Drain the fat from the vegie mixture and let it cool.
- Place the wrappers onto a smooth surface.
- Divide the veggie mixture in the center of each wrapper evenly.
- Roll the wrappers around the filling and with your cornstarch mixture, brush the edges and press to seal completely.
- In a large cast-iron skillet or deep fryer, heat the oil and reduce the heat to low.
- Carefully, add the rolls in the skillet in batches.

- Fry the rolls for about 2-3 minutes or till golden brown and transfer onto paper towel lined plates to drain.
- Serve these rolls with the sauce of your choice.

Amount per serving: 1

Timing Information:

Preparation	30 mins
Total Time	42 mins

Nutritional Information:

Calories	62.2
Cholesterol	1.4mg
Sodium	178.0mg
Carbohydrates	10.6g
Protein	1.9g

* Percent Daily Values are based on a 2,000 calorie diet.

Sweet Pumpkin Spring Rolls

Ingredients

- 1 (15-oz.) can pumpkin puree
- 1/4 C. sugar
- 1/4 C. honey
- 2 eggs
- 1 tsp fresh ginger, grated finely
- 2 tsps ground cinnamon
- 1 tsp ground cardamom
- Salt, to taste
- 1/2 tsp almond extract
- 1 (16-oz.) package spring rolls
- 2-3 tbsps canola oil
- Powdered sugar, as required

Directions

- In a large bowl, mix together the pumpkin puree, sugar, honey, ginger, spices and almond extract and refrigerate, covered for about 2 hours.
- Set your oven to 350 degrees F before doing anything else.
- Place the wrappers onto a smooth surface.
- Divide the pumpkin mixture in the center of each wrapper evenly.
- Roll the wrappers around the filling and with your cornstarch mixture, brush the edges and press to seal completely.
- Coat the rolls with oil evenly and arrange in a baking dish in a single layer.
- Cook everything in the oven for about 15 minutes or till golden brown.
- Serve these rolls with a sprinkling of powdered sugar.

Amount per serving: 12

Timing Information:

Preparation	10 mins
Total Time	25 mins

Nutritional Information:

Calories	192.7
Cholesterol	38.6mg
Sodium	278.8mg
Carbohydrates	34.9g
Protein	5.2g

* Percent Daily Values are based on a 2,000 calorie diet.

Cheesy Beef Spring Rolls with Honey Mustard Sauce

Ingredients

For Sauce:

- 1/2 C. ketchup
- 1 1/2 tbsps honey
- 1 1/2 tbsps Dijon mustard
- 1/3 tsp cayenne pepper

For Rolls:

- 1/4 C. olive oil
- 1 1/2 lbs beef top loin, trimmed and chopped
- 1/4 lb provolone cheese, cut into 1/2-inch pieces
- 1/3 lb American cheese, cut into 1/2-inch pieces
- Salt and freshly ground black pepper, to taste
- 8 (9 1/2-inch) spring roll wrappers
- 6 egg yolks, beaten lightly
- Vegetable oil, as required

Directions

- In a large bowl, add all the sauce ingredients and mix till well combined and keep aside.
- In a large skillet, heat olive oil on medium heat and cook the beef for about 5-7 minutes or till browned.
- Drain off the liquid from the skillet and stir in both cheese.

- Cook for about 2-3 minutes or till the cheeses melt completely.
- Stir in the salt and black pepper and remove everything from the heat and let it cool completely.
- Place the wrappers onto a smooth surface and coat the surface of the wrapper with egg yolk evenly.
- Divide the beef mixture in the center of each wrapper evenly.
- Fold the inner sides of the wrappers around the filling and roll tightly.
- In a large cast-iron skillet or deep fryer, heat the oil to 350 degrees F.
- Carefully, add the rolls in the skillet in batches.
- Fry the rolls for about 8 minutes or till golden brown and transfer onto paper towel lined plates to drain.
- Cut each roll in half and serve with sauce.

Amount per serving: 4

Timing Information:

Preparation	25 mins
Total Time	55 mins

Nutritional Information:

Calories	622.8
Cholesterol	297.4mg
Sodium	1314.7mg
Carbohydrates	48.2g
Protein	24.1g

* Percent Daily Values are based on a 2,000 calorie diet.

Pork & Crab Spring Rolls

Ingredients

- 1/4 lb large lump crabmeat
- 6-oz. ground pork
- 1 large egg, beaten
- 1 scallion, chopped finely
- 1 tbsp fresh ginger, minced
- 2 small garlic cloves, minced
- 1/4 C. fresh cilantro, chopped
- Salt, to taste
- 30 rice paper wedges
- 1 egg yolk, beaten
- 6 C. peanut oil

Directions

- In a large bowl, add all the ingredients except rice papers, egg yolk and oil and mix till well combined.
- Soak the rice papers, one at a time in a bowl of warm water till soft and transfer onto paper towels.
- Place the rice papers onto a smooth surface.
- Divide the chicken mixture in the center of each rice paper evenly.
- Roll the rice papers around the filling and with egg yolk brush the edges and press to seal completely.
- In a large cast-iron skillet or deep fryer, heat the oil to 365 degrees F.
- Carefully, add the rolls to the skillet in batches.
- Fry the rolls for about 5-6 minutes or till golden brown and transfer onto paper towel lined plates to drain.

Amount per serving: 1

Timing Information:

Preparation	30 mins
Total Time	2 hrs 30 mins

Nutritional Information:

Calories	407.2
Cholesterol	20.1mg
Sodium	39.5mg
Carbohydrates	0.2g
Protein	2.2g

* Percent Daily Values are based on a 2,000 calorie diet.

Chicken, Shrimp & Veggie Spring Rolls

Ingredients

- 3 tbsps olive oil, divided
- 2 (6-oz.) skinless, boneless chicken breasts, minced
- 1/2 lb shrimp, peeled, deveined and chopped
- 6 dried shiitake mushrooms, soaked in boiling water, covered for 20 minutes, drained, stemmed and chopped
- 4 baby carrots, chopped finely
- 3 scallions, chopped
- 1 C. mug bean sprouts
- 1 tbsp fresh gingerroot, minced
- 1 1/2 tbsps garlic, minced
- 1 tbsp fresh mint leaves, chopped
- 2 tbsps fresh cilantro, chopped
- 2-oz. cellophane noodles, soaked in boiling water, covered for 20 minutes, drained and chopped
- 1 tbsp fish sauce
- 1 tbsp soy sauce
- 1 tsp sugar
- Salt, to taste
- 15 (8-inch) spring roll wrappers
- Vegetable oil, as required

Directions

- Set your oven to 425 degrees F before doing anything else.
- In a large skillet, heat 2 tbsps of olive oil and cook the chicken for about 5 minutes or till browned.

- Stir in the shrimp and cook for about 1 1/2 minutes and transfer into a large bowl to cool.
- In the same skillet, heat the remaining olive oil and cook the mushrooms, carrots and scallions and stir fry for about 4 minutes.
- Stir in the bean sprouts, ginger, garlic and fresh herbs and stir fry for about 1 minute.
- Remove everything from the heat and discard all the liquid.
- In the bowl of chicken mixture, add cooked vegetables, noodles, sauces and salt and mix till well combined.
- Place the wrappers onto a smooth surface.
- Divide the chicken mixture in the center of each wrapper evenly.
- Roll the wrappers around the filling and with your wet fingers brush the edges and press to seal completely.
- Coat the rolls with vegetable oil evenly and arrange in a large baking sheet in a single layer.
- Cook everything in the oven for about 20 minutes or till golden brown.

Amount per serving: 1

Timing Information:

Preparation	20 m
Total Time	30 m

Nutritional Information:

Calories	82.0
Cholesterol	32.8mg
Sodium	280.6mg
Carbohydrates	10.7g
Protein	8.1g

* Percent Daily Values are based on a 2,000 calorie diet.

Cabbage & Carrot Spring Rolls

Ingredients

- 1 tbsp peanut oil
- 2 green onions, chopped
- 2 garlic cloves, minced
- 2 carrots, peeled and chopped finely
- 1 head green cabbage, cored and chopped
- 2 tbsps stir-fry sauce
- 1/8 tsp cayenne pepper
- 1/4 tsp freshly ground white pepper
- 2 tbsps rice wine
- 20-25 spring roll wrappers
- Oil, as required

Directions

- In a large skillet, heat peanut oil on medium heat and sauté green onion, garlic and carrot for about 5 minutes. Add cabbage, stir-fry sauce and both peppers and cook for about 15 minutes. Stir in the wine and cook till just absorbed. Remove everything from the heat and keep aside to cool completely. Place the wrappers onto a smooth surface.
- Divide the veggie mixture in the center of each wrapper evenly.
- Fold the inner sides of the wrappers around the filling and roll tightly.
- In a large cast-iron skillet or deep fryer, heat the oil.
- Carefully, add the rolls in the skillet in batches.
- Fry the rolls till golden brown and transfer onto paper towel lined plates to drain.

Amount per serving: 20

Timing Information:

Preparation	30 mins
Total Time	45 mins

Nutritional Information:

Calories	47.2
Cholesterol	0.7mg
Sodium	81.8mg
Carbohydrates	8.2g
Protein	1.5g

* Percent Daily Values are based on a 2,000 calorie diet.

Chicken & Ham Spring Rolls

Ingredients

- 1 garlic clove, minced
- 1/4 tsp five-spice powder
- 1/4 tsp freshly ground black pepper
- 2 chicken breasts, lbed thinly
- 2 tbsps milk
- 1 egg
- 2 large ham slices
- Flour, as required
- 2 spring roll wrappers
- Oil, as required

Directions

- In a bowl, mix together garlic, five-spice powder and black pepper.
- Sprinkle the chicken breasts with the garlic mixture evenly.
- In a shallow dish, place flour.
- In another shallow dish, add milk and egg and beat well.
- Place 1 rolled ham slice over each chicken breast and roll the breasts tightly.
- Coat the chicken rolls in flour evenly and discard the extra.
- Now, dip the chicken rolls in egg mixture evenly and shake off the extra.
- Place the wrappers onto a smooth surface.
- Arrange the chicken roll diagonally over the spring roll wrappers and roll the wrappers around the chicken roll and with some egg mixture, brush the edges and press to seal completely.
- In a large cast-iron skillet or deep fryer, heat the oil.

- Carefully, add the rolls in the skillet in batches.
- Fry the rolls till golden brown and transfer onto paper towel lined plates to drain.

Amount per serving: 4

Timing Information:

Preparation	20 mins
Total Time	35 mins

Nutritional Information:

Calories	160.5
Cholesterol	94.3mg
Sodium	90.2mg
Carbohydrates	3.1g
Protein	17.3g

* Percent Daily Values are based on a 2,000 calorie diet.

Herbed Tuna Spring Rolls with Tangy Sauce

Ingredients

- 500 g tuna, sashimi grade
- 1 tbsp wasabi paste
- 2 tbsps coriander leaves
- 2 tbsps chopped fresh parsley
- 8 spring roll wrappers
- oil, to deep fry
- 2 tbsps lime juice
- 2 tbsps soy sauce

Directions

- In a shallow dish, mix together the herbs.
- Coat each tuna piece with wasabi paste and roll into herb mixture evenly.
- Place the wrappers onto a smooth surface.
- Place the tuna pieces in the center of each wrapper evenly.
- Roll the wrappers around the filling and with your wet fingers brush the edges and press to seal completely.
- In a large cast-iron skillet or deep fryer, heat the oil.
- Carefully, add the rolls in the skillet in batches.
- Fry the rolls for about 30-45 seconds or till golden brown and transfer onto paper towel lined plates to drain.
- Meanwhile in a bowl, mix together soy sauce and lime juice.
- Serve the rolls with sauce.

Amount per serving: 1

Timing Information:

Preparation	15 mins
Total Time	20 mins

Nutritional Information:

Calories	117.2
Cholesterol	24.4mg
Sodium	322.1mg
Carbohydrates	5.2g
Protein	15.8g

* Percent Daily Values are based on a 2,000 calorie diet.

Veggie & Thread Noodles Spring Rolls with Mustard Sauce

Ingredients

For Rolls:

- 2 tbsps extra-virgin olive oil
- 2 scallions, sliced thinly
- 1/2 tbsp fresh ginger, minced
- 1 tbsp garlic, minced
- 1 lb mixed wild mushrooms
- 1 carrot, peeled and grated
- 2 C. Napa cabbage, shredded
- 1 tbsp oyster sauce
- 1 tbsp hoisin sauce
- 1/2 C. bean sprouts
- 2-oz. bean thread noodles, blanched and chopped
- 2 tbsps fresh cilantro, chopped
- Salt and freshly ground black pepper, to taste
- Spring roll wrappers
- 1 egg beaten
- Vegetable oil, as required

For Sauce:

- 1/2 C. Dijon mustard
- 1/4 C. rice vinegar
- 1/4 C. hot water
- 1 tbsp sugar
- 1 tsp sesame oil, toasted

Directions

- In a large skillet, heat olive oil on medium-high heat and sauté scallion, ginger and garlic for about 1 minute.

- Add cabbage, stir-fry sauce and both peppers and cook for about 15 minutes.
- Stir in the mushrooms and stir fry them for about 1 minute.
- Stir in the carrot and cabbage and stir fry them for about 2 minutes.
- Stir in the sauces and immediately remove from heat.
- Remove everything from the heat and immediately, stir in bean sprouts, noodles, salt and black pepper and keep aside to cool.
- Place the wrappers onto a smooth surface.
- Divide the veggie mixture in the center of each wrapper evenly.
- Roll the wrappers around the filling and with your wet fingers brush the edges and press to seal completely.
- In a large cast-iron skillet or deep fryer, heat the oil to 350 degrees F.
- Carefully, add the rolls in the skillet in batches.
- Fry the rolls for about 2 minutes or till golden brown and transfer onto paper towel lined plates to drain.
- In a large bowl, add all the sauce ingredients and mix till the sugar dissolves.
- Cut each roll in half and serve with sauce.

Amount per serving: 1

Timing Information:

Preparation	20 m
Total Time	30 m

Nutritional Information:

Calories	91.6
Cholesterol	21.2mg
Sodium	231.6mg
Carbohydrates	11.4g
Protein	3.1g

* Percent Daily Values are based on a 2,000 calorie diet.

Salmon Spring Rolls with Spicy Mayo

Ingredients

For Mayo:

- 1 C. mayonnaise
- 1 tbsp fresh lime juice
- 2 tbsps chili paste
- Salt and freshly ground black pepper, to taste

For Rolls:

- 1 1/2 lbs boneless salmon fillets, cut into small chunks
- 1/4 C. fresh gingerroot, minced
- 1/4 C. garlic, minced
- 1/2 of bunch fresh cilantro, chopped
- 2 tbsps flour
- Canola oil, as required

Directions

- For the mayo, in a bowl, add all the ingredients and beat till well combined and keep aside.
- In a large bowl, mix together salmon, ginger, garlic and cilantro.
- In a small bowl, mix together flour and enough water to form a paste.
- Place the wrappers onto a smooth surface.
- Divide the salmon mixture in the center of each wrapper evenly.
- Roll the wrappers around the filling and with flour mixture, brush the edges and press to seal completely.
- In a large cast-iron skillet or deep fryer, heat the oil to 350 degrees F.

- Carefully, add the rolls to the skillet in batches.
- Fry the rolls for about 3-4 minutes or till golden brown and transfer onto paper towel lined plates to drain.
- Serve these rolls with mayo.

Amount per serving: 4

Timing Information:

Preparation	3 m
Total Time	50 m

Nutritional Information:

Calories	507.2
Cholesterol	105.3mg
Sodium	627.6mg
Carbohydrates	30.7g
Protein	37.2g

* Percent Daily Values are based on a 2,000 calorie diet.

Sausage Rolls in Sweet Nutty Glaze

Ingredients

- 1 (8-oz.) can refrigerated crescent dinner rolls
- 24 cocktail smoked sausage links
- 3 tbsps brown sugar
- 3tbsps honey
- 1/2 C. nuts, chopped
- 1/2 C. butter, melted

Directions

- Set your oven to 400 degrees F before doing anything else.
- Separate the dinner rolls into triangles by unrolling the dough and cut into three triangles lengthwise.
- Place the dough triangles onto a smooth surface.
- Arrange a sausage link over each triangle and tightly roll them.
- In an 11x7x2-inch baking dish, add the remaining ingredients and mix till well combined.
- Carefully, place rolls, seam side down in glaze.
- Cook everything in the oven for about 15-20 minutes or till golden brown.

Amount per serving: 24

Timing Information:

Preparation	20 mins
Total Time	40 mins

Nutritional Information:

Calories	221.6
Cholesterol	41.5mg
Sodium	514.4mg
Carbohydrates	10.3g
Protein	6.7g

* Percent Daily Values are based on a 2,000 calorie diet.

Indian Spring Rolls

Ingredients

- 1/2 C. cornflour
- 1 C. refined flour
- 1 C. paneer, Grated
- 1 egg, Lightly Beaten
- 1 pinch black pepper
- 1 bunch spring onion, Chopped
- 1 C. oats
- 2 tsps red chili powder
- water, as required
- oil, for fry
- salt

Directions

- In a bowl, add flours, egg, salt and water and beat till a thin batter forms.
- In another bowl mix together remaining ingredients except oil.
- In a pan, heat a little oil and add enough flour mixture to make a thin sheet.
- Immediately, transfer onto paper towel lined plates.
- Repeat with the remaining mixture.
- Divide the paneer mixture in the center of each egg sheet evenly.
- Fold the inner sides of egg sheets around the filling and roll tightly.
- In a large cast-iron skillet or deep fryer, heat the oil on medium heat.
- Carefully, add the rolls in the skillet in batches.
- Fry the rolls till golden brown and transfer onto paper towel lined plates to drain.

Amount per serving: 3

Timing Information:

Preparation	15 mins
Total Time	35 mins

Nutritional Information:

Calories	455.6
Cholesterol	62.0mg
Sodium	56.2mg
Carbohydrates	82.8g
Protein	16.8g

* Percent Daily Values are based on a 2,000 calorie diet.

Spicy Beef Spring Rolls

Ingredients

- 2 tbsps olive oil
- 1 medium onion, chopped
- 1 lb lean ground beef
- 1 tbsp fresh ginger, minced
- 3 garlic cloves, minced
- 1 tsp chili paste
- 1/4 C. soy sauce
- Salt and freshly ground black pepper, to taste
- 1 head green cabbage, cored and shredded
- 2 medium carrots, peeled and grated
- 3 scallions, slice thinly
- 1 tbsp fresh lime juice
- 1 (14-oz.) package spring roll wrappers
- 1/2 C. oil

Directions

- In a large skillet, heat olive oil and sauté onion till tender.
- Add beef and cook for about 1-2 minutes.
- Add ginger, garlic, chili paste, soy sauce, salt and black pepper and cook for about 10-15 minutes.
- Add cabbage and cook for about 5-10 minutes.
- Stir in the carrots and stir fry till all the liquid is absorbed.
- Stir in the scallion and lemon juice and stir fry for about 1 minute and Remove everything from the heat to cool.
- Place the wrappers onto a smooth surface.

- Divide the beef mixture in the center of each wrapper evenly.
- Roll the wrappers around the filling and with your wet fingers brush the edges and press to seal completely.
- In a large cast-iron skillet, heat the oil.
- Carefully, add the rolls to the skillet in batches.
- Fry the rolls till golden brown and transfer onto paper towel lined plates to drain.

Amount per serving: 20

Timing Information:

Preparation	5 min
Total Time	15 min

Nutritional Information:

Calories	177.9
Cholesterol	16.5mg
Sodium	401.6mg
Carbohydrates	15.9g
Protein	7.7g

* Percent Daily Values are based on a 2,000 calorie diet.

Beef & Carrot Spring Rolls

Ingredients

- 2 tbsps olive oil
- 1/2 of onion, chopped
- 2 garlic cloves, minced
- 1 lb ground beef
- 2 medium carrots, peeled and chopped
- 1 beef bouillon
- 2 tbsps soy sauce
- Salt and freshly ground black pepper, to taste
- 25 spring roll wrappers
- 1/4 C. water
- 1 tbsp cornstarch
- Oil, as required

Directions

- In a large skillet, heat olive oil and sauté the onion and garlic till tender.
- Add the beef and cook till browned. Add the carrots, beef bouillon, soy sauce, salt and black pepper and cook till desired doneness.
- Drain off the excess oil and remove everything from the heat and keep aside to cool. Place the wrappers onto a smooth surface. Divide the beef mixture in the center of each wrapper evenly. Roll the wrappers around the filling and with cornstarch mixture, brush the edges and press to seal completely.
- In a large cast-iron skillet or deep fryer, heat the oil to 350 degrees F.
- Carefully, add the rolls in the skillet in batches.
- Fry the rolls till golden brown and transfer onto paper towel lined plates to drain.

Amount per serving: 6

Timing Information:

Preparation	10 mins
Total Time	40 mins

Nutritional Information:

Calories	323.2
Cholesterol	54.4mg
Sodium	692.6mg
Carbohydrates	24.1g
Protein	18.4g

* Percent Daily Values are based on a 2,000 calorie diet.

Cinnamon Apple Spring Rolls with Coffee Sauce

Ingredients

For Sauce:

- 1 C. cream cheese, softened
- 1 (10 1/4-oz.) can condensed milk
- 1 tbsp coffee

For Rolls:

- 1/2 C. butter
- 1/2 C. brown sugar
- 2 C. apples, peeled and cubed
- 2 tbsps flour, mixed with a little water
- 1 tsp ground cinnamon
- 10 spring roll wrappers

Directions

- For the sauce in a blender, add all the ingredients and pulse till well combined and refrigerate to chill before serving.
- In a pan, melt the butter on medium heat and add the sugar and apples.
- Cook, stirring occasionally till the apples become tender.
- Stir in the flour mixture and cinnamon till well combined.
- Remove everything from the heat and let it cool completely.
- Place the wrappers onto a smooth surface.
- Divide the apple mixture in the center of each wrapper evenly.

- Roll the wrappers around the filling and with your wet fingers brush the edges and press to seal completely.
- In a large cast-iron skillet or deep fryer, heat the oil.
- Carefully, add the rolls in the skillet in batches.
- Fry the rolls till golden brown and transfer onto paper towel lined plates to drain.
- Serve these rolls with coffee.

Amount per serving: 5

Timing Information:

| Preparation | 15 mins |
| Total Time | 30 mins |

Nutritional Information:

Calories	1101.1
Cholesterol	169.2mg
Sodium	536.4mg
Carbohydrates	143.3g
Protein	20.3g

* Percent Daily Values are based on a 2,000 calorie diet.

Pumpkin Egg Rolls with Creamy Filling

Ingredients

For Rolls:

- 1 1/2 C. flour
- 1 1/2 tsps baking powder
- 1 1/2 tsps ground ginger
- 3 tsps ground cinnamon
- 3/4 tsp ground nutmeg
- Salt, to taste
- 2 eggs
- 3 egg whites
- 1 1/2 C. sugar
- 1 1/2 tsps fresh lemon juice
- 1 1/3 C. pumpkin puree

For Filling:

- 8-oz. fat-free cream cheese, softened
- 1 C. fat-free cool whip

Directions

- Set your oven to 375 degrees F before doing anything else and grease and flour a jelly roll pan.
- In a large bowl, mix together flour, baking powder, spices and salt and sift well.
- In another bowl, add eggs and egg whites and beat well.
- Slowly, add sugar, beating continuously.
- Add lemon juice and pumpkin puree.
- Add the pumpkin mixture into the flour mixture and mix till well combined.
- Transfer the flour mixture on the prepared pan evenly.

- Cook everything in the oven for about 15 minutes.
- Transfer the cake onto a paper towel and roll together and keep aside to cool.
- Meanwhile in a bowl, add filling ingredients and beat till well combined.
- Carefully, unroll the cake.
- Spread the cream cheese mixture over the cake evenly.
- Roll again and refrigerate to chill before serving.
- Cut the cake roll into 12 equal sized slices and serve.

Amount per serving: 12

Timing Information:

Preparation	10 mins
Total Time	25 mins

Nutritional Information:

Calories	193.6
Cholesterol	32.5mg
Sodium	318.3mg
Carbohydrates	39.8g
Protein	6.3g

* Percent Daily Values are based on a 2,000 calorie diet.

Cheesy Chicken Spring Rolls

Ingredients

- 1 lb skinless, boneless chicken breast
- 1 bouillon cube
- 1/2 C. mozzarella cheese, shredded
- 3/4 C. hot sauce
- 1 (12-oz.) package spring roll wrappers
- 6 C. peanut oil
- 1 egg
- 1 tbsp water
- 1/2 C. blue cheese salad dressing
- 6 celery ribs, sliced into sticks

Directions

- In a pan of boiling water, add chicken breast and bouillon cube and cook till done completely.
- Drain well and transfer into a large bowl to cool and chop into bite-sized pieces.
- Add the cheese and hot sauce and mix till well combined.
- Place the wrappers onto a smooth surface.
- Divide the chicken mixture in the center of each wrapper evenly.
- In a small bowl, add egg and water and beat till well combined.
- Roll the wrappers around the filling and with egg mixture, brush the edges and press to seal completely.

- In a large cast-iron skillet or deep fryer, heat the oil to 350 degrees F.
- Carefully, add the rolls in the skillet in batches.
- Fry the rolls till golden brown and transfer onto paper towel lined plates to drain.
- Serve these rolls with blue cheese dressing and celery sticks.

Amount per serving: 1

Timing Information:

| Preparation | 25 mins |
| Total Time | 35 mins |

Nutritional Information:

Calories	596.6
Cholesterol	26.6mg
Sodium	385.4mg
Carbohydrates	9.0g
Protein	5.9g

* Percent Daily Values are based on a 2,000 calorie diet.

Mango & Veggie Spring Rolls with Creamy Sauce

Ingredients

For Sauce:

- 1/3 C. peanut butter
- 3 tbsps brown sugar
- 3 tbsps soy sauce
- 1 tbsp sesame oil
- 1 tsp rice vinegar
- Sriracha chili sauce, to taste
- Salt, to taste

For Rolls:

- Cellophane noodles
- 1 tbsp sugar
- 1 tbsp rice vinegar
- 1 avocado, peeled, pitted and sliced
- Fresh lime juice
- 1 mango, peeled, pitted and sliced
- 1 carrot, peeled and shredded
- 1 C. lettuce, shredded
- Chopped fresh cilantro
- Chopped fresh basil leaves
- Rice paper sheets

Directions

- For the sauce, in a microwave safe bowl, mix together all the ingredients and microwave on high for 30 seconds or till smooth.
- If sauce is too thick then stir in a little water.

- Cook the cellophane noodles according to the package's directions, and rinse under cold water and drain.
- In a bowl, add noodles, sugar and vinegar and toss to coat well.
- In a second bowl, add avocado and drizzle with lime juice
- In a third bowl, mix together remaining ingredients except rice papers.
- Soak the rice papers, one at a time in a bowl of warm water till soft and transfer onto paper towels.
- Place the rice papers onto a smooth surface.
- In the center of each rice paper, place the noodles, followed by the avocado and mango mixture.
- Fold the inner sides of the wrappers around the filling and roll tightly.
- Cut each roll in half and serve with sauce.

Amount per serving: 6

Timing Information:

| Preparation | 30 m |
| Total Time | 50 m |

Nutritional Information:

Calories	249.6
Cholesterol	0.0mg
Sodium	590.3mg
Carbohydrates	27.7g
Protein	6.3g

* Percent Daily Values are based on a 2,000 calorie diet.

Spring Roll Noodle Salad with Shrimp

Ingredients

For Shrimp:

- 1 tsp red curry paste
- 1 tsp vegetable oil
- 1 tsp sugar
- Pinch of salt
- 3/4 lb shrimp, peeled and deveined
- Cooking oil, as required

For Dressing:

- 1 tbsp fresh gingerroot, minced
- 2 tbsps sugar
- 3 tbsps fresh lime juice
- 2 tbsps vegetable oil
- 2 tsps chili-garlic sauce
- 2 tsps fish sauce

For Salad:

- 2-oz. dry rice noodles
- 1/2 C. cucumber, seeded, halved lengthwise and sliced thinly
- 1/2 C. carrot, peeled and julienned
- 1/2 C. red bell pepper, seeded and chopped
- 1/2 C. fresh bean sprouts
- 3 C. iceberg lettuce, torn
- 1/4 C. fresh mint leaves, chopped
- 1/4 C. fresh cilantro, chopped

Directions

- For the shrimp in a large bowl, mix together all the ingredients except cooking oil and refrigerate to marinate for about 15 minutes.

- For the dressing in a bowl, add the dressing ingredients and beat till well combined and keep aside.
- In a large bowl of boiling water, add the noodles for about 3-4 minutes or till soft.
- Drain the noodles and rinse under cold water and transfer into a large bowl.
- Add vegetables and stir to combine.
- In a large skillet, heat cooking oil on medium-high heat and sear the shrimp for about 5 minutes or till done.
- For serving, place noodles mixture into serving plates evenly and top with shrimp.
- Drizzle with dressing and serve with the topping of chopped peanuts and fried wonton wrapper strips.

Amount per serving: 2

Timing Information:

Preparation	20 mins
Total Time	40 mins

Nutritional Information:

Calories	485.4
Cholesterol	214.5mg
Sodium	1602.7mg
Carbohydrates	54.0g
Protein	27.3g

* Percent Daily Values are based on a 2,000 calorie diet.

Chocolaty Banana Spring Rolls

Ingredients

- 8 large spring roll wrappers
- 2-oz. unsalted butter, melted
- 4 small ripe bananas, peeled, sliced lengthwise and halved diagonally
- 4-oz. bittersweet chocolate, chopped
- Salt, to taste

Directions

- Set your oven to 425 degrees F before doing anything else and line a baking dish with parchment paper.
- Arrange 2 wrappers onto a smooth surface and coat with some butter.
- Arrange one piece of banana over the lower third of the wrapper.
- Top with chocolate and sprinkle with salt.
- Fold the inner sides of wrapper around the banana and roll tightly.
- Repeat with the remaining wrappers and banana pieces.
- Arrange the rolls on the prepared baking dish in a single layer and coat with the butter.
- Cook everything in the oven for about 5-7 minutes or till golden brown.

Amount per serving: 8

Timing Information:

| Preparation | 20 mins |
| Total Time | 27 mins |

Nutritional Information:

Calories	119.0
Cholesterol	15.9mg
Sodium	47.0mg
Carbohydrates	16.1g
Protein	1.3g

* Percent Daily Values are based on a 2,000 calorie diet.

Spicy Beef & Shrimp Spring Rolls

Ingredients

- 1 tbsp olive oil
- 1 garlic, minced
- 2-oz. beef, chopped
- 2-oz. shrimp, peeled, deveined and chopped
- 2-oz. carrots, peeled and julienned
- 2 1/2-oz. zucchini, julienned
- 1-oz. squash, julienned
- 2 tsps chili sauce
- 2-oz. cellophane noodles, soaked in boiling water, covered for 5 minutes, drained and chopped
- 2 tsps oyster sauce
- 2 tsps water
- 1 1/2 tsps cornstarch
- 32 rice paper sheets
- Oil, as required

Directions

- In a skillet, heat the oil and sauté the garlic for a few seconds.
- Stir in the beef and shrimp and cook till browned.
- Stir in the veggies, chili sauce and oyster sauce and remove from heat.
- Let the beef mixture cool and mix in the noodles.
- Soak the rice papers, one at a time in a bowl of warm water till soft and transfer onto paper towels.
- Place the rice papers onto a smooth surface.
- In the center of each rice paper, place the beef mixture evenly.

- In a small bowl, mix together water and cornstarch.
- Roll the wrappers around the filling and with the cornstarch mixture, brush the edges and press to seal completely.
- In a large cast-iron skillet or deep fryer, heat the oil to 325 degrees F.
- Carefully, add the rolls to the skillet in batches.
- Fry the rolls till golden brown and transfer onto paper towel lined plates to drain.

Amount per serving: 4

Timing Information:

Preparation	15 mins
Total Time	20 mins

Nutritional Information:

Calories	143.6
Cholesterol	36.3mg
Sodium	549.1mg
Carbohydrates	19.0g
Protein	7.3g

* Percent Daily Values are based on a 2,000 calorie diet.

Creamy Turkey Lettuce Rolls

Ingredients

- 1/2 tsp prepared mustard
- 3-oz. low-fat cream cheese, softened
- 1/2 lb cooked turkey, sliced thinly
- 6 large lettuce leaves
- 1 carrot, peeled and grated

Directions

- In a bowl, add mustard and cream cheese and beat till well combined.
- Spread the mustard mixture over each turkey slice.
- Divide the turkey slices over the lettuce leaves evenly and roll and secure with a tooth pick.
- Serve with a garnishing of carrot.

Amount per serving: 6

Timing Information:

Preparation	10 mins
Total Time	10 mins

Nutritional Information:

Calories	104.5
Cholesterol	36.2mg
Sodium	90.4mg
Carbohydrates	2.1g
Protein	9.4g

* Percent Daily Values are based on a 2,000 calorie diet.

Tangy Chicken, Apple & Veggie Spring Rolls

Ingredients

For Chicken:

- 2 tsps fresh ginger, minced
- 3 garlic cloves, minced
- 1 small fresh red chili pepper, minced
- 3 tbsps fresh orange juice
- 1 tbsp cooking wine
- 1 tbsp low-sodium soy sauce
- 1/2 lb skinless, boneless chicken breast, cut into thin strips
- 1 tbsp canola oil

For Rolls:

- 1 large apple, peeled, cored and cut into thin strips
- 1 small red bell pepper, seeded and cut into thin strips
- 4 green onions (green part), sliced
- 1 1/2 tsps sesame oil
- 1 tbsp seasoned rice vinegar
- 12 round rice paper sheets
- 1 head Boston lettuce, leaves separated

Directions

- Set the broiler of the oven and grease a large cooking sheet.
- For the chicken in a bowl, add all the ingredients except the canola oil and toss to coat and refrigerate, covered for at least 15 minutes.
- Just before cooking, drain the liquid.

- In a skillet, heat the canola oil and stir fry chicken for about 2-3 minutes.
- Transfer the chicken into a bowl and let it cool.
- Add the apple, vegetables, sesame oil and vinegar and stir to combine.
- Soak the rice papers, one at a time in a bowl of warm water till soft and transfer onto paper towels.
- Place the rice papers onto a smooth surface.
- In the center of each rice paper, place the beef mixture evenly.
- Roll the wrappers around the filling and with your wet fingers brush the edges and press to seal completely.
- Arrange the rolls onto the prepared baking sheet in a single layer and coat each roll with a little oil.
- Cook everything under the broiler for about 8-10 minutes per side or till golden brown.
- Wrap each lettuce in a lettuce leaf and serve with your favorite sauce.

Amount per serving: 1

Timing Information:

| Preparation | 30 mins |
| Total Time | 55 mins |

Nutritional Information:

Calories	56.6
Cholesterol	11.0mg
Sodium	64.6mg
Carbohydrates	4.6g
Protein	4.9g

* Percent Daily Values are based on a 2,000 calorie diet.

Braised Eggplant Rolls

Ingredients

For Pancakes:

- 1 C. flour, sifted
- 1 C. boiling water
- 2 tbsps sesame oil
- 1/2 C. sesame seeds

For Eggplants:

- 2 tbsps peanut oil
- 4 garlic cloves, minced
- 2 tsps fresh ginger, minced
- 4-5 narrow Japanese eggplants, cut into small pieces
- 1 tbsp oyster sauce
- 1 tbsp oyster sauce
- 1 tbsp brandy
- 1 tsp sugar
- 4 spring onions, sliced thinly
- 1/2 of cucumber, seeded and julienned

Directions

- In a bowl, add the flour and slowly, add water, mixing till a smooth dough forms.
- Place the dough onto a floured surface and with your hands, knead the dough for at least 3 minutes.
- With plastic wrap, cover the dough and keep aside for about 30 minutes.
- In a shallow dish, place sesame oil sand in another dish, add the sesame seeds.
- Divide the dough into 18 equal sized portions and shape each into a ball.

- Take 2 balls at a time and roll the slightly.
- Coat 1 ball with sesame oil and place another ball on top.
- Roll this combo of 2 balls in sesame seeds evenly and roll out to a pancake.
- Repeat with the remaining dough, oil and sesame seeds.
- Heat a large nonstick skillet on medium heat and cook the pancakes, one at a time for about 1-2 minutes per side.
- Meanwhile for the eggplants in a skillet, heat the oil on medium heat and stir in garlic, ginger and eggplant.
- Reduce the heat to low and stir fry for about 5 minutes.
- Stir in the sauces, brandy and sugar and cook, covered for about 10 minutes.
- Place the eggplant mixture over the warm pancakes and serve alongside spring onions and cucumber.

Amount per serving: 4

Timing Information:

Preparation	15 mins
Total Time	1 hr

Nutritional Information:

Calories	612.1
Cholesterol	0.0mg
Sodium	393.8mg
Carbohydrates	89.1g
Protein	16.5g

* Percent Daily Values are based on a 2,000 calorie diet.

Cheesy Asparagus Bread Spring Rolls

Ingredients

- Poppy seeds, as required
- 10 fresh white bread slices, crust removed
- 2-oz. cream cheese, softened
- 1 egg yolk
- 1/4 C. mayonnaise
- 1/4 C. old cheddar cheese, grated
- 1/2 tsp fresh lemon zest, grated finely
- 20 cooked thin asparagus stalks
- 2 tbsps butter, melted

Directions

- Set your oven to 400 degrees F before doing anything else.
- Sprinkle the poppy seeds over one side of the bread slices.
- With a rolling pin, flatten the slices and flip the side and roll again.
- In a bowl, add cream cheese, egg yolk and mayonnaise and beat till well combined. Add cheddar cheese and lemon zest and stir to combine.
- Place the bread slices onto a smooth surface, plain side upwards.
- Spread the cream cheese mixture over the plain side evenly and top with 2 asparagus stalks.
- Roll the slices around asparagus and cut each roll in half.
- Coat the slices with melted butter evenly and arrange onto a large baking sheet in a single layer.
- Cook everything in the oven for about 10 minutes.

Amount per serving: 20

Timing Information:

Preparation	20 mins
Total Time	30 mins

Nutritional Information:

Calories	87.1
Cholesterol	18.1mg
Sodium	141.6mg
Carbohydrates	9.6g
Protein	3.1g

* Percent Daily Values are based on a 2,000 calorie diet.

Vegan Spring Rolls with Tangy Sauce

Ingredients

For Sauce:

- 1/4 C. fresh lime juice
- 2 tsps Thai fish sauce
- 1 tsp dark sesame oil
- 1 garlic clove, minced
- 1 tsp fresh ginger, minced
- 2 tbsps fresh cilantro, chopped
- 3 tbsps sugar
- Pinch of red pepper flakes, crushed

For Rolls:

- 1 tsp canola oil
- 1 tsp fresh ginger, minced
- 1 garlic clove, minced
- 1 onion, sliced
- 1/2 lb savory cabbage, shredded
- 1 tbsp low-sodium soy sauce
- 2-oz. rice noodles
- 2 tsps dark sesame oil
- 1/2 C. carrot, peeled and grated
- 16 (6-inch round) rice papers

Directions

- For the sauce in a bowl, mix together all the ingredients and keep aside.
- In a large skillet, heat the oil on medium heat and sauté the ginger and garlic for about 1 minute.
- Stir in the onion, cabbage and soy sauce and increase the heat to medium-high.

- Cook, stirring occasionally for about 15 minutes and transfer the mixture into a bowl.
- Meanwhile in a large bowl of hot water, soak the rice noodles for about 10 minutes.
- Drain and rinse under cold water and cut the noodles into small pieces with kitchen shears.
- Add cooked rice noodles, sesame oil and carrot in the bowl with cabbage mixture and stir to combine.
- Soak the wrappers, one at a time in a bowl of warm water till soft and transfer onto paper towels.
- Place the rice papers onto a smooth surface.
- Divide the rice noodles mixture in the center of each wrapper evenly.
- Fold the inner sides of the wrappers around the filling and roll tightly.

Amount per serving: 8

Timing Information:

Preparation	15 mins
Total Time	45 mins

Nutritional Information:

Calories	86.0
Cholesterol	0.0mg
Sodium	211.8mg
Carbohydrates	15.7g
Protein	1.3g

* Percent Daily Values are based on a 2,000 calorie diet.

Shrimp & Rice Noodles Spring Rolls

Ingredients

- 4-oz. rice noodles
- 1/4 lb large shrimp, peeled and deveined
- 16 spring roll wrappers
- 1 avocado, peeled, pitted and sliced thinly
- 1 red bell pepper, seeded and sliced thinly
- 8 large fresh basil leaves, chopped

Directions

- In a pan of boiling water, cook the rice noodles according to the package's directions.
- Drain and rinse under cold water and cut the noodles into small pieces with kitchen shears.
- Meanwhile in another pan of boiling water, cook the shrimp for about 60-90 seconds or till just done completely.
- Drain well and immediately, place in a bowl of chilled water.
- Drain well and cut the shrimp lengthwise.
- Soak the wrappers, one at a time in a bowl of warm water till soft and transfer onto paper towels.
- Place the wrappers onto a smooth surface.

- In the center of each wrapper, place the shrimp, followed by avocado, rice noodles, bell peppers and basil evenly.
- Fold the inner sides of the wrappers around the filling and roll tightly.
- Cut each roll in half and serve with the sauce of your choice.

Amount per serving: 1

Timing Information:

Preparation	25 mins
Total Time	30 mins

Nutritional Information:

Calories	81.9
Cholesterol	10.3mg
Sodium	106.7mg
Carbohydrates	12.9g
Protein	2.5g

* Percent Daily Values are based on a 2,000 calorie diet.

Steamed Tempeh & Veggie Spring Rolls

Ingredients

- 2 tsps sesame oil, toasted
- 8-oz. tempeh, cut into thin strips
- 1/2 of roasted red bell pepper, seeded and cut into thin strips
- 1/2 C. Chinese cabbage, shredded
- 1/2 C. bean sprouts
- 4 scallions, chopped
- 2 tbsps fresh lemon juice
- 8 egg roll wraps

Directions

- In a skillet, heat the oil on medium heat and cook tempeh till browned completely.
- Remove everything from the heat and transfer onto paper towel lined plates to drain.
- In a bowl, mix together vegetables and lemon juice.
- Place the wrappers onto a smooth surface.
- In the center of each wrapper, place the veggie mixture, followed by tempeh.
- Roll the wrappers around the filling and with your wet fingers brush the edges and press to seal completely.
- In a steamer basket over boiling water, place wrappers and steam for about 10 minutes.
- Transfer onto paper towel lined plates to drain.

Amount per serving: 1

Timing Information:

Preparation	20 mins
Total Time	30 mins

Nutritional Information:

Calories	166.3
Cholesterol	2.8mg
Sodium	187.8mg
Carbohydrates	23.2g
Protein	8.8g

* Percent Daily Values are based on a 2,000 calorie diet.

Soy Sauce Tuna Spring Rolls

Ingredients

- 1 garlic clove, minced
- 2 tbsps thick soy sauce
- 2 tsps sesame oil
- 2 lbs tuna, cut into strips
- Salt and freshly ground black pepper, to taste
- 25 spring roll wrappers
- Peanut oil, as required

Directions

- In a bowl, mix together garlic, soy sauce and sesame oil.
- Add the tuna strips and coat with the garlic mixture generously and sprinkle with salt and black pepper.
- Place the wrappers onto a smooth surface.
- Divide the tuna mixture in the center of each wrapper evenly.
- Roll the wrappers around the filling and with your wet fingers brush the edges and press to seal completely.
- In a large cast-iron skillet or deep fryer, heat the oil.
- Carefully, add the rolls to the skillet in batches.
- Fry the rolls till golden brown and transfer onto paper towel lined plates to drain.

Amount per serving: 1

Timing Information:

| Preparation | 15 mins |
| Total Time | 30 mins |

Nutritional Information:

Calories	84.2
Cholesterol	15.9mg
Sodium	61.3mg
Carbohydrates	4.6g
Protein	10.1g

* Percent Daily Values are based on a 2,000 calorie diet.

Chocolaty Peanut Spring Rolls

Ingredients

- 2 tbsps butter
- 1/2 C. heavy cream
- 6-oz. semisweet chocolate, chopped
- 1/2 C. peanuts
- 12 egg roll wraps
- Vegetable oil, as required
- Powdered sugar

Directions

- In a pan, add butter and cream on medium-high heat and bring to a boil.
- Remove everything from the heat and immediately, sprinkle with chocolate and keep aside for about 1 minute. With a whisk, beat till chocolate is combined and stir in peanuts. Cover and refrigerate to chill for at least 1 hour.
- Place the wrappers onto a smooth surface.
- Divide the chocolate mixture in the center of each wrapper evenly.
- Roll the wrappers around the filling and with your wet fingers brush the edges and press to seal completely.
- Arrange the rolls in a baking dish and refrigerate, covered with plastic wrap before serving.
- In a large cast-iron skillet or deep fryer, heat the oil to 350 degrees F.
- Carefully, add the rolls in the skillet in batches.
- Fry the rolls for about 1 minute per side or till golden brown and transfer onto paper towel lined plates to drain. Serve with a sprinkling of sugar if you like.

Amount per serving: 12

Timing Information:

Preparation	20 mins
Total Time	28 mins

Nutritional Information:

Calories	249.8
Cholesterol	21.5mg
Sodium	204.9mg
Carbohydrates	24.0g
Protein	6.7g

* Percent Daily Values are based on a 2,000 calorie diet.

Chicken & Mushroom Spring Rolls

Ingredients

- 1 tbsp vegetable oil
- 2 (5-oz.) skinless, boneless chicken breasts, cut into 1/4-inch pieces
- 1 tbsp Chinese five-spice powder
- 1 tbsp light soy sauce
- 3-oz. bean sprouts
- 1 carrot, peeled and sliced thinly
- 4 dried Chinese mushrooms, soaked in hot water for 20 minutes and drained
- 2 scallions, sliced thinly
- 1 (1-inch) piece fresh ginger, grated
- 1 garlic clove, minced
- 12 spring roll wrappers
- 1 tbsp water
- 1 tbsp cornstarch
- 3 C. peanut oil

Directions

- In a skillet, heat vegetable oil on high heat and sear the chicken for about 2-3 minutes.
- Stir in five-spice powder and soy sauce and Remove everything from the heat and keep aside to cool.
- In a large bowl, mix together cooked chicken and vegetables.
- Arrange the 2 wrappers over each other onto a smooth surface.
- Divide the chicken mixture in the center of each wrapper evenly.

- In a small bowl, mix together water and cornstarch.
- Roll the wrappers around the filling and with the cornstarch mixture, brush the edges and press to seal completely.
- In a large cast-iron skillet or deep fryer, heat the oil to 375 degrees F.
- Carefully, add the rolls in the skillet in batches.
- Fry the rolls for about 3-5 minutes or till golden brown and transfer onto paper towel lined plates to drain.

Amount per serving: 1

Timing Information:

Preparation	20 m
Total Time	50 m

Nutritional Information:

Calories	1090.8
Cholesterol	24.2mg
Sodium	375.8mg
Carbohydrates	15.1g
Protein	11.8g

* Percent Daily Values are based on a 2,000 calorie diet.

Sweetcorn & Crab Spring Rolls with Sweet & Spicy Sauce

Ingredients

For the spring rolls

- 3 tbsps vegetable oil
- 1 shallot, chopped
- 1 garlic clove, chopped
- 8 oz. white crab meat
- 1 tbsp fresh cilantro, chopped
- 1/3 C. creme fraiche
- 1 lime, juice and zest of
- 3 oz. canned sweetcorn
- 12 spring roll wrappers
- 1 egg, beaten
- 1 pinch salt & freshly ground black pepper
- 1 pint vegetable oil, for deep-frying

For the dipping sauce

- 3 oz. superfine sugar
- 2 red chilies
- 2 egg tomatoes
- 8 kaffir lime leaves
- 2 stalks lemongrass, finely chopped
- 1 oz. fresh gingerroot, peeled
- 2 garlic cloves
- 2 shallots, peeled
- 2 tbsps fish sauce
- 3 tsps sesame oil
- 3 tsps dark soy sauce
- 2 tbsps clear honey
- 3 limes, juice and zest of

Easy Spring Roll Cookbook

Directions

- In a frying pan, heat the oil and sauté the garlic and shallot till just softened.
- Transfer the shallot mixture into a bowl and let it cool completely.
- Add crab meat, sweetcorn, crème fraiche, cilantro, lime zest, lime juice, salt and black pepper and stir to combine.
- Place the wrappers onto a smooth surface.
- Divide the crab meat mixture in the center of each wrapper evenly.
- Roll the wrappers around the filling and with beaten egg, brush the edges and press to seal completely.
- In a large cast-iron skillet or deep fryer, heat the oil to 375 degrees F.
- Carefully, add the rolls in the skillet in batches.
- Fry the rolls till golden brown and transfer onto paper towel lined plates to drain.
- Meanwhile in a pan, melt the sugar on medium heat and cook till sugar becomes caramelized.
- Meanwhile in a blender, add the remaining sauce ingredients and pulse till a puree forms.
- Add the puree in the pan with the caramelized sugar and bring to a boil and cook, stirring gently for about 5 minutes.
- Serve these rolls with sauce.

Amount per serving: 4

Timing Information:

Preparation	40 mins
Total Time	1 hr

Nutritional Information:

Calories	1472.3
Cholesterol	112.1mg
Sodium	1753.5mg
Carbohydrates	58.9g
Protein	18.2g

* Percent Daily Values are based on a 2,000 calorie diet.

Strawberry & Orange Spring Rolls with Strawberry Sauce

Ingredients

For Rolls:

- 4 1/2-oz. raw sugar
- 4 eggs
- 4 1/2-oz. unsalted butter
- Fresh juice and zest of 3 oranges
- Oil, as required
- 2 lbs fresh strawberries, hulled and chopped finely
- 8 spring roll sheets
- 2 tsps arrowroot powder
- 1 egg white

For Sauce:

- Chopped fresh strawberries, as required
- 3 3/4-oz. caster sugar
- 2 fluid oz. water
- 2 fluid oz. Grand Mariner

Directions

- For the rolls in a bowl, add raw sugar and eggs and beat till well combined and keep aside.
- In a pan, mix together butter, orange zest and orange juice and bring to a gentle simmer.

- Slowly, add the egg mixture, stirring continuously till the mixture becomes thick.
- Remove everything from the heat and let it cool completely.
- In a bowl, mix together the chopped strawberries and 1 1/2 tbsps of orange mixture.
- In a small bowl, mix together the arrowroot powder and egg white.
- Place the wrappers onto a smooth surface.
- Divide the strawberry mixture in the center of each wrapper evenly.
- Roll the wrappers around the filling and with your cornstarch mixture, brush the edges and press to seal completely.
- In a large cast-iron skillet or deep fryer, heat the oil.
- Carefully, add the rolls in the skillet in batches.
- Fry the rolls till golden brown and transfer onto paper towel lined plates to drain.
- Meanwhile for the sauce in a pan, mix together all the ingredients and simmer till strawberries become soft.
- Transfer the mixture into a blender and pulse till a puree forms.
- Serve the rolls with strawberry sauce.

Amount per serving: 4

Timing Information:

| Preparation | 30 mins |
| Total Time | 45 mins |

Nutritional Information:

Calories	733.2
Cholesterol	281.5mg
Sodium	183.7mg
Carbohydrates	105.6g
Protein	12.1g

* Percent Daily Values are based on a 2,000 calorie diet.

FILIPINO STYLE SPRING ROLLS

Ingredients

For Filling:

- 8-oz. shrimp, peeled, deveined and chopped
- 8-oz. ground pork
- 1/4 C. celery, chopped finely
- 1/4 C. carrot, peeled and chopped finely
- 3 tbsps white onion, chopped
- 1 garlic clove, minced
- 1/4 C. fresh parsley, chopped finely
- 1 egg, beaten slightly
- 1 tbsp soy sauce
- 1 tsp sugar
- Salt, to taste
- Pinch of freshly ground black pepper

For Rolls:

- Spring roll wrappers
- Oil, as required

For Sauce:

- 2/3 C. water
- 1/4 C. apple cider vinegar
- 2 tbsps fish sauce
- 1/4 C. sugar
- 1 tsp cornstarch

Directions

- In a large cast-iron skillet or deep fryer, heat the oil to 375 degrees F.
- For the filling, in a large bowl, mix together all the ingredients.
- Divide the filling mixture in the center of each wrapper evenly.

- Roll the wrappers around the filling and with your wet fingers brush the edges and press to seal completely.
- Carefully, add the rolls in the skillet in batches.
- Fry the rolls till golden brown and transfer onto paper towel lined plates to drain.
- Meanwhile for the sauce in a pan, add all the ingredients on high heat and beat till the sugar dissolves.
- Bring to a boil and cook till the desired thickness.
- Serve the wrappers with sauce.

Amount per serving: 12

Timing Information:

Preparation	30 mins
Total Time	35 mins

Nutritional Information:

Calories	92.8
Cholesterol	43.6mg
Sodium	5.8g
Carbohydrates	5.8g
Protein	92.8

* Percent Daily Values are based on a 2,000 calorie diet.

Veggie Spring Rolls with Spicy Sauce

Ingredients

For Sauce:

- 1 1/2 tbsps sugar
- 3 tbsps rice wine vinegar
- 1 tbsp sesame oil, toasted
- 1 tbsp soy sauce
- 3/4 tsp chili-garlic sauce

For Rolls:

- 10 (8 1/2-inch) rice papers rounds
- 3 carrots, peeled and julienned
- 2 cucumbers, julienned
- 2 red bell peppers, seeded and cut into thin strips
- Fresh chopped cilantro leaves
- Fresh chives, blanched

Directions

- For the sauce, in a bowl, mix together all the ingredients and refrigerate, covered till chilled.
- Soak the rice papers, one by one in a bowl of warm water till soft and transfer onto paper towels.
- Place the rice papers onto a smooth surface.
- In the center of each rice paper, place the vegetables and cilantro evenly.
- Fold the inner sides of the wrappers around the filling and roll tightly.
- Cut the rolls in half and with a piece of chive, tie the each rolls.
- Serve these rolls with sauce.

Amount per serving: 20

Timing Information:

Preparation	45 mins
Total Time	4 hrs 45 mins

Nutritional Information:

Calories	21.5
Cholesterol	0.0mg
Sodium	57.4mg
Carbohydrates	3.6g
Protein	0.4g

* Percent Daily Values are based on a 2,000 calorie diet.

Strawberry & Banana Spring Rolls

Ingredients

- 12 large square rice paper sheets
- 8 medium strawberries, hulled and sliced
- 2 bananas, peeled and sliced
- 7-oz. strawberry flavored vegan soy yogurt
- Fresh mint leaves, for garnishing

Directions

- Soak the rice papers, one by one in a bowl of warm water till soft and transfer onto paper towels.
- Place the rice papers onto a smooth surface.
- Divide the strawberry and banana slices in the center of each rice paper evenly.
- Fold the inner sides of wrappers around the filling and roll tightly.
- Cut each roll in half and serve with yogurt and a garnishing of mint.

Amount per serving: 4

Timing Information:

Preparation	10 mins
Total Time	20 mins

Nutritional Information:

Calories	60.1
Cholesterol	0.0mg
Sodium	0.8mg
Carbohydrates	15.3g
Protein	0.8g

* Percent Daily Values are based on a 2,000 calorie diet.

THANKS FOR READING! NOW LET'S TRY SOME **SUSHI** AND **DUMP DINNERS**....

http://bit.ly/2443TFg

To grab this **box set** simply follow the link mentioned above, or tap the book cover.

This will take you to a page where you can simply enter your email address and a PDF version of the **box set** will be emailed to you.

I hope you are ready for some serious cooking!

<u>http://bit.ly/2443TFg</u>

You will also receive updates about all my new books when they are free.

Also don't forget to like and subscribe on the social networks. I love meeting my readers. Links to all my profiles are below so please click and connect :)

<u>Facebook</u>

<u>Twitter</u>

Come On...
Let's Be Friends :)

I adore my readers and love connecting with them socially. Please follow the links below so we can connect on Facebook, Twitter, and Google+.

Facebook

Twitter

I also have a blog that I regularly update for my readers so check it out below.

My Blog

Can I Ask A Favour?

If you found this book interesting, or have otherwise found any benefit in it. Then may I ask that you post a review of it on Amazon? Nothing excites me more than new reviews, especially reviews which suggest new topics for writing. I do read all reviews and I always factor feedback into my newer works.

So if you are willing to take ten minutes to write what you sincerely thought about this book then please visit our Amazon page and post your opinions.

Again thank you!

Interested in Other Easy Cookbooks?

Everything is easy! Check out my Amazon Author page for more great cookbooks:

For a complete listing of all my books please see my author page.

Printed in Great Britain
by Amazon